KINGDOM LIVING

KINGDOM LIVING

*Growing in the
Character of Christ*

John Wimber

VINE
BOOKS

Servant Publications
Ann Arbor, Michigan

Cover design by Charles Piccirilli
Cover photo-illustration with sand by Lawrence Fitton

Vine Books is an imprint of Servant Publications
especially designed to serve Evangelical Protestants.

Published by Servant Books
P.O. Box 8617
Ann Arbor, Michigan 48107

87 88 89 90 91 10 9 8 7 6 5 4 3 2 1

Printed in the United States of America
ISBN 0-89283-361-0

KINGDOM LIVING

Kingdom Living: Growing in the Character of Christ

At the height of the Jesus people movement back in the sixties, I became a Christian. I wasn't a hippie, but I was a rock and roll musician, and so I was on the fringe of the hippie community, in which the Jesus people movement had such a powerful impact.

I was fortunate to be led to Christ and greatly influenced by a man who clearly understood the seriousness and high cost of the gospel. He taught us that there was no such thing as "cheap grace." The call to discipleship meant living fully for God, living lives of righteousness and faith that would be examples of word and deed to a world desperately in need of salvation.

But after only two years my mentor moved away, and as time went by we came under the influence of a more popular version of the "gospel," one presented by many that was a bit deficient. Its basic message was, "Come and escape reality. Accept Jesus and get ready for the Rapture, because he's coming back any day now."

For a while I became passive, waiting for the Rapture. I must have been waiting patiently for at least three weeks when it began to dawn on me that what I had learned in the first two years of my Christian walk still applied to my life: I was supposed to be *doing* something while I waited. Maybe there was more to being a Christian than I had thought.

I now know that the "something" that all of us are supposed to be doing is growing into the image and likeness of Christ, growing in Christian character. Over the course of more than twenty years in the ministry, I have become convinced that one of the most important things any of us can do as a Christian is to *grow up before we grow old.* It is absolutely essential, if we are to make progress in the great enterprise of helping men and women find redemption, that we see growth toward maturity as part of our goal—both for them and for ourselves.

From the World to the Kingdom

Christ gives us power and authority to go and make *disciples,* men and women who have a personal relationship with Christ, a relationship of trust and dependence, of giving oneself fully to God.

Being a disciple means more than just making a decision for Jesus and waiting for his Second Coming; it involves changing—turning from sin, the flesh, and the devil and becoming like Christ. It is a conversion *from* the world *to* the kingdom of God.

C. Peter Wagner describes mature disciples as having these characteristics:

—They are fully incorporated into the body of Christ (a local church).

—They have been taught the basics of the word of God.

—They have been trained in a Christian way of life.

—They are able and willing to do Christ's works on earth.

Disciples, then, are changed in every area of their lives: from the way they think about God, crea-

tion, morality, and decision-
making to their attitudes toward
themselves and people around
them, to their way of dealing with
emotions like anger, fear, ambi-
tion, and selfishness. The fruit of
the spirit—"love, joy, peace,
patience, kindness, goodness,
faithfulness, gentleness, and self-
control" (Gal 5:22-3)—now forms
their character, which conforms to
Christ's character.

In other words, we are to
become just like Jesus. And we are
to become like him *in this lifetime.*
That's the will of God for each one
of us. And what God commands,
he enables. Apart from his help,
we could never become like Jesus.
With his help, we have every pos-
sibility and every probability of
growing into Christlikeness here
on earth.

The Father sent the Holy Spirit
to empower and guide us, to give
us his gifts that we might do

Christ's works. And he sent his Spirit to dwell in us, to change us into Christ's likeness, to cultivate the fruit of the Spirit. As we cooperate with his work in us, we become more like Jesus, growing in the Spirit's fruit.

Growing Fruit

Too often Christians focus on gifts—natural and supernatural—and ignore character. But this bypasses a fundamental principle of the Christian life: gifts and abilities, no matter how magnificent, are either limited or enhanced by Christian character. In this regard, John Blattner, in his book, *Growing in the Fruit of the Spirit,* describes character as a multiplying factor:

It [character] multiplies, for good or ill, the effects of our gifts. Give a spiritual gift to a

person of average character—
let's rate it a 'one'—and he is
likely to exercise it in a responsible fashion. The same gift in
the hands of someone with a
much stronger and better-
formed character—say, a 'five'—
will be five times more effective.

Of course, the principle works
the other way around, too. You
probably remember from high
school mathematics that any
figure multiplied by zero equals
zero. Even an impressive and
dramatic talent is wasted if the
character of the person using it
is weak. Then, of course, there
are the 'negative numbers.' This
reflects the harmful impact of a
talented person using his gifts
for distorted ends.

I find this phenomenon to be
very widespread among Christians. In fact, it was a great stum-
bling block to me in coming into

the power of the Holy Spirit. One of the main reasons I used to resist speaking in tongues was that I didn't like a lot of the tongues-speakers I had met!

Gifts are to character as adornments are to a body. Beautiful adornments—jewelry, fine clothing, and so on—look good on a beautiful body. But when the body has been neglected and has itself become unattractive, you can do almost anything to it—jewel it, perfume it, deck it out in gorgeous clothes—and it still doesn't look right.

So it is with spiritual gifts. They are to be adornments to a well-formed character, which is the foundation for properly displaying them. Thus we are to seek the *fruit* of the Spirit as a precursor to seeking the *gifts* of the Spirit.

An important characteristic of fruit is that it *grows*, going through a process of development that culminates in maturity. Fruit doesn't grow to maturity in one day; it goes through a process of development in which both internal factors (its genetic makeup) and external factors (water, soil, temperature) combine to create maturity.

It is the same for Christians. We too go through a process of character formation in which the fruit of the Spirit grows to maturity in us. With the Holy Spirit living in us, we have the "genetic makeup" to reflect God's nature. But initial conversion does not ensure Christian maturity. We must be willing to submit patiently to and cooperate aggressively with the process of discipleship, understanding that there are no shortcuts to maturity.

Many times we are impatient with this process, and we seek to cut it short. I often find people seeking to achieve maturity through either "magic" or "structure."

Now, these people are definitely onto something real. They are seeking happiness and fulfillment in their Christian lives. But they have not yet learned to equate that fulfillment with the completion of a process of growth.

Some of them want to have "the magic wand of prayer" waved over them, as though by laying hands on them and uttering the right combination of syllables we could transform them into spiritual supersaints, able to leap tall problems in a single bound.

Others come seeking structure: the right set of spiritual disciplines, the right methods and techniques, that will catapault them into spiritual maturity.

Now, both prayer and structure *do* play some role in the process of growth. But neither is complete in itself. Many people experience great liberation and forward momentum as a result of prayer ministry, but we cannot simply "pray in" complete and total Christian maturity.

Likewise, spiritual disciplines and methods can move us ahead a great deal. But they can be somewhat deceptive. A new technique or approach will often seem fabulously effective—for a while. But once the novelty wears off, it remains effective only as we continue to pursue it patiently over a long period of time. Anyone who has ever gone on a diet will be familiar with the phenomenon: for the first few days weight loss is rapid and relatively effortless. Then we reach a plateau, and progress toward our weight goal comes more slowly.

I have seen this principle played out in my own spiritual life recently. About a year ago, my wife and I sensed the Lord calling us to more regular and vigorous intercessory prayer on behalf of he churches we are connected with. The first few months were glorious. Every morning we rose early and met with God. It was dynamic. It was exciting. I was beginning to suspect that I just might be one of the best pray-ers in the entire body of Christ.

Lately, it has been more like drudgery. I can't get up on time. I can't stay awake once I do get up. Something inside me seems to scream, "This is stupid! God may not even be awake yet! Why am I dragging myself out of bed like this?" Some mornings it feels as though all I'm doing is sitting in a chair and dribbling coffee into my beard. If I were counting on structure to move my spiritual life ahead, I'd have given up on this particular piece of structure long ago. But I knew that I must continue in morning prayers. Why? Because God told me to! Obedience has its own reward.

We need to come to grips with the reality that there are no short-cuts. Growth in character is a process, one that happens one day at a time, one step at a time.

What are the key elements of the process of character formation? What are those elements of spiritual life with which we can actively cooperate with the Holy Spirit?

The Turning Point

The most fundamental element in character formation is basic conversion, turning from self to a personal relationship with God through faith in Jesus Christ.

John Wesley, the great English theologian and evangelist, described his own conversion as a "heart-warming experience": "I felt

I did trust in Christ—Christ alone for salvation. And an assurance was given me that he had taken away *my* sins—even *mine*—and saved *me* from the law of sin and death." Jesus came into John Wesley's life, and through him the Paraclete, the Helper, gained access to his heart, mind, and soul. John Wesley was never to be the same, for a new "life principle" was in him.

In Scripture this is called new birth, a birth into the kingdom of God. This is the point at which kingdom seed is planted deeply in our souls. "You have been born anew," wrote Peter, "not of perishable seed but of imperishable, through the living and abiding word of God" (1 Pt 1:23).

All of our efforts in character formation are worthless if the seed of the kingdom has not first been planted in us.

From Glory to Glory

After conversion we grow in Christ's character as we behold God. "And we all," wrote Paul, "with unveiled face, beholding the glory of the Lord, are being changed into his likeness from one degree of glory to another" (2 Cor 3:18).

The "glory to glory" principle of character growth is based in part on the principle of association: the more time we spend with someone, the more we become like him. This is especially true during developmental stages of life. This is clearly seen in father-son or mother-daughter relationships where often, especially when the relationship has been healthy, the child grows up to be like the parent, reflecting the same mannerisms, voice inflection, temperament.

I spent many of my formative years living with my grandfather, and one of my strongest memories of childhood is the feeling of wanting to grow up to be "just like Grandpa." He made his living trading and training horses, and as you might imagine he was a rather rough, crude sort of fellow. I can still remember being with him when he was looking over some horse he was interested in. I'd stand right behind him, putting my hands on my hips just like he did, spitting and snarling and scratching just like he did. He was my ideal at that age.

Later on, the man who led me to Christ also became a role model for me. He had gone through some very difficult circumstances, which were part of the "refiner's fire" in his spiritual development and which produced in him a remarkably strong character. Gunner (that was his nickname) was a terrific evangelist, and my first exposure to Christian ministry came as I followed him around, watching him and listening to him and learning how he shared the gospel. I got to know all his illustrations, all his stories, all his jokes—I could almost tell them better than he did. It wasn't long before I was able to go off on my own and do the same kind of work myself, all because I had emulated this man and his ministry.

So it is with following the Lord. We become more like him as we spend time with him, emulating him in all things.

Keys to the Kingdom

New Christians are called "babes," dependent on their Father for spiritual growth. The more time they spend with God, the more they become like him. The ways we do this are familiar:

—Worship: the highest honor that we have in the kingdom of God is the worship of the Father. Through praise and adoration we grow closer to God, learning of his holiness and, in turn, growing in holiness. This one discipline is perhaps the most important means of character growth, because we sacrifice who we are to adore who he is. In our death to self, we open ourselves to his life-transforming power.

—Prayer: daily prayer involves both talking and listening. Prayer is not primarily an exercise of asking for what we want, it is asking what God wants. As we learn more of his will for our lives, we grow in his nature and holiness.

And we learn that we can trust God. I think the biggest lesson my wife and I have learned in the months since God called us to more vigorous intercession is that God hears and answers our prayers no matter how sleepy or distracted or unspiritual we may feel when we pray them.

—Scripture study: the Bible is the word of God; it tells us who God is, how he acts, what he expects of us. As we grow in knowledge of the Bible, we grow in the knowledge of God—and are transformed more and more into his likeness. Our goal is not simply to memorize scripture or understand it intellectually (helpful as these activities are), but to be changed by it. God's word is alive and active. As we submit ourselves to it inwardly, it produces a change in us outwardly.

—Corporate life: being a Christian involves participation in a body of believers, brothers and sisters in the new covenant. As we worship, pray, study Scripture, and fellowship together, not only does God reveal more and more of who he is to us, but "iron sharpens iron," and God uses others to mature us.

We haven't been called to a "solo flight" for God. We've been called to a corporate life. We're called to grow and develop in and with one another.

Knowledge v. Obedience

Western Christians often assume that if they *understand* a truth of the Christian life, it is truly a part of their lives. They equate growth in knowledge about God with growth in God's character. This is a mistaken notion.

One of the great tragedies of Western Christendom is the disparity between what Christians say they believe and how they actually live. Much of the power and authority of kingdom witness is undermined by Christians who are not living what they profess.

While we must learn about who

God is and how he acts, it is of little value unless it affects our behavior. In this regard, obedience to what God teaches is a key element in the process of character building. In fact, disobedience severely limits our ability to know God's word. This was Christ's point in rebuking the experts in the law in Luke 11:46, 52: "Woe to you, because you load people down with burdens they can hardly carry, and you yourselves will not lift one finger to help them. . . . Woe to you experts in the law, because you have taken away the key to knowledge. You yourselves have not entered, and you have hindered those who were entering." There is grave danger in separating belief and behavior: the danger of losing the revelation God has already given us.

As we imitate Christ, choosing to live like him in every way possible, we grow in his character. This is an active choice in which we are always asking, How would Jesus do this? What would Christ have said in this situation? What was Jesus' attitude when encountering this type of person? All the time we are conscious that Christ is our model, our ideal, our ultimate discipler.

Being "Otherly"

"Therefore be imitators of God," Paul sums up in Ephesians 5:1-2, "as beloved children. And walk in love, as Christ loved us and gave himself up for us, a fragrant offering and sacrifice to God." Paul was especially concerned that we imitate Christ's love, that his way of sacrifice be evident in our lives also.

This text exemplifies what I call being "otherly," that is, being oriented more to the service of others than to the service of ourselves. We must learn to abandon our own predilections, the things we desire, the safety, the security, the happiness—things that are good in themselves but that must be set aside for the sake of growth in Christ.

Many times, in talking with Christians about struggles and difficulties they were experiencing, I have said, "If you have to have both success and Jesus, you may have trouble in this life. If you have to have both a perfect marriage and Jesus, you may be in for a hard time. If you have to have both human comfort and Jesus, you may find yourself traveling a rough road."

I say this not because there is anything wrong with success, perfect marriages, or human happiness. I say it because anytime we make *anything* other than Jesus our portion in life, we open the door to frustration. I can confidently assure you that if you *do* make Jesus your portion, you'll *get* Jesus—and much more besides. But everything else has to be secondary.

Loving others and personal sacrifice are not only a key to the *process* of character formation but also represent the *goal* of character formation. I should not have to write this, but too frequently I encounter Christians wanting the benefits of the kingdom—a clear conscience, eternal life, prosperity, a feeling of joy—while eschewing kingdom responsibilities. They are unwilling to say no to the world; they attempt to harmonize sin with Scripture. But it doesn't work. And inevitably it leads to ruin.

Christians who never learn to say no to the flesh are like babies who mess their diapers and cry constantly. When a three-month-old baby behaves this way, it is understandable. Parents are not overjoyed about messy diapers, but they care for their children knowing that a better day is coming, one in which their children will have self-control and concern for others. But when a ten-, twenty-, or thirty-year-old continues to act this way, when he or she hasn't learned how to love brothers and sisters and sacrifice personal appetites for God's desires—when there has been no character growth—it is a great tragedy for the person, for God, and for God's people.

Christ is our chief model of Christian maturity, but Scripture indicates that older brothers and sisters can also be models of Christian character. For example, in 1 Corinthians 4:15-16 we read, "Even though you have ten thousand guardians in Christ, you do not have many fathers, for in Christ Jesus I became your father through the gospel. *Therefore I urge you to imitate me.*" Paul is not teaching that he takes the place of Jesus, that he is equal with the Father. Rather, Paul encourages the Corinthian Christians to look to him as a model of how they should live, to what they should aspire as brothers and sisters.

That Paul would make such a statement is encouraging. He is saying that maturity is within the grasp of all believers, that though we will never be perfected until the fullness of the kingdom in the age to come, we can have substantial growth and maturity in this lifetime.

The Refiner's Fire

In the midst of giving praise to God for our hope in Christ, Peter offers this insight into trials:

In this [our hope in Christ] you greatly rejoice, though now for a little while you may have had to suffer grief in all kinds of trials. These have come so that your faith—of greater worth than gold, which perishes even though refined by fire—may be proved genuine and may result in praise, glory, and honor when Jesus Christ is revealed. (1 Pt 1:6-7)

Even though Peter is writing primarily to a group of Christians undergoing a particular instance of persecution, the principle he gives applies universally. The fact is, we're all going to "get it." I've never known anyone who got through life without pain, difficulty, and hardship.

I've seen people who have developed all kinds of messages and models for victorious Christian living. I've seen people holding all kinds of positive faith orientations that say, "If you'll just follow this approach, claim these passages, learn these teachings, you will indeed become a spiritual superman, able to leap tall problems in a single bound."

But my experience over the years, as I've considered these approaches, studied Scripture, and examined the evidence of what actually goes on in the world, is that everybody "gets it." Everyone has problems in their personal lives, or in their families, or in their careers. It doesn't matter how positive they are or how much they focus on certain teachings or passages.

In fact, it is my conviction that God not only *allows* such trials to come our way, but that he even *sends* us difficulty from time to time as part of his process of strengthening and purifying us.

Blessings alone will not produce the fruit he's looking for. He has to include some trials in order to achieve his ends in our lives. Often it is precisely the difficulties and trials that produce the highest quality return for the Lord. Often it is pain that makes us willing (even eager!) to learn, to change, to grow.

Thus we find ourselves, on the one hand, on a great pilgrimage toward the promised land, toward the fullness of life in the kingdom of heaven. But at the same time that God is about the business of getting us into heaven, he is also about the business of *getting heaven into us.*

Peter teaches that we grow in Christian character through the tests that adverse circumstances bring to our lives. We are refined, made pure in our motives, attitudes, and service. We are made stronger in faith. All this is to fulfill

Christ's goal of creating new men and women to reflect his character.

In James 1:2, we read that we should "Consider it pure joy . . . whenever [we] face trials of many kinds." Why? "Because . . . the testing of [our] faith develops perseverance" (v. 3). Trials, then, are an integral element in the character formation process.

The forty-eighth chapter of Jeremiah contains an instructive illustration of what it means for God to take an active role in unsettling and resettling our lives:

> Moab has been at rest from youth,
>> like wine left on its dregs,
> not poured from one jar to another—
>> she has not gone into exile.
> So she tastes as she did,
>> and her aroma is unchanged.
> "But days are coming,"

declares the Lord,
"when I will send men who pour
   from jars,
   and they will pour her out;
they will empty her jars
   and smash her jugs." (Jer
48:11-12)

The imagery refers to the process of wine-making in the ancient world. During the period of fermentation and aging, a kind of sediment would filter down and collect at the bottom of the wine jar. This was called "the dregs." If the wine was allowed to sit on the dregs too long, it would become bitter and polluted. So the wine-maker would, from time to time, pour the wine from one jar to another, leaving more and more of the dregs behind.

Perhaps you have met people who refused to let the Lord pour them from bottle to bottle, who have resisted his efforts to change and rearrange their circumstances. The taste and aroma of their lives becomes bitter. It's the same way with you and me. The circumstances of our life produce sediment, and if we wallow in them too long, we can become bitter. Even when the prospect seems painful, we must learn not to resist when God seeks to further our growth through trials.

The writer of Hebrews, writing about discipline ("For what son is not disciplined by his father?"), clearly states that trials are allowed for us to grow: "No discipline seems pleasant at the time, but painful. Later on, however, it produces a harvest of righteousness and peace for those who have been trained by it" (12:7, 11). We are actually *trained* by trials and discipline.

The obvious implication is that we should not be surprised when trouble comes. Trouble is promised in Scripture. Peter says as much in his letter: "Dear friends, do not be surprised at the painful trial you are suffering, as though something strange were happening to you. But rejoice . . ." (1 Pt 4:12-13). Rejoice. Consider it all joy. Welcome the trials that come.

I suspect that very few of us have reached the place where we honestly and truly rejoice at trials. "Oh, how wonderful! The tire is flat!" But we miss out on so much when we avoid or run from the challenges and tests that are placed before us for the testing, strengthening, and proving of our character. Only when they have had their effect on us can we be effective representatives of the kingdom of God.

In the book of Exodus we read of the Israelites coming to the waters of Marah. They didn't want to drink from these waters, because they tasted bitter and apparently produced a condition similar to dysentery. But the fact was that those waters were part of God's provision for the Israelites. In the days that followed they suffered from a loss of strength that might have been avoided had they allowed the waters of Marah to do their work.

Again, the point is that you and I need to learn to accept even the bitter-tasting things that come to us from God, trusting that he knows what he's doing, and that our momentary discomfort is designed to equip and strengthen us for challenges yet to be faced.

The more we want to grow, the more we should expect trials. This is a hard word in a culture that so highly values ease and comfort, prosperity and self-fulfillment. But looking to our model, Jesus Christ, we observe that trials marked every step of his life, culminating in the cross.

Is character formation in the kingdom of God worth all the trouble? Are personal sacrifice and discipline, bearing up under trials, obedience to the point of loss of reputation and fortune, worth the cost? The answer is yes! "Blessed is the man who endures trial, for when he has stood the test he will receive the crown of life which God has promised to those who love him" (Jas 1:12).

Kingdom Character

What are some of the marks of someone who successfully cooperates with Christ in the discipleship process? Though not a complete list, the following are indicators of mature Christian character:

1. A mature Christian is a servant. He does nothing out of a desire for selfish gain, understanding that the mark of a servant is that he be submitted to God's will. He doesn't do things *for* God; rather, he does things *under* God. And he expects nothing in return for his service. When people disappoint (as they surely will), the servant of God picks himself up, turns to God, praises him for his grace, and asks him for the next set of orders.

2. A mature Christian deals with his sin before the Lord. As Paul said, "I always take pains to have a clear conscience toward God and toward men" (Acts 24:16). Repentance requires humility toward God and, when we have wronged them, toward brothers and sisters. It also requires knowing how to receive forgiveness when God extends it to us, resulting in a clear conscience, an appropriate self-image, and humility. Because of this, a mature Christian is marked by righteousness, by behavior that avoids even the appearance of wrongdoing.

3. A mature Christian is honest and open in his dealings with brothers and sisters. He is able to be candid with others, sharing what God is doing in his life, not fearful of admitting failure or weakness.

4. A mature Christian brings personal difficulties to the Lord. Instead of running from painful situations or personal defeats and weaknesses, he faces them squarely, bringing them before God and asking for his help. Honestly facing these difficulties will many times allow them to be turned to victories; in all instances God will use them to further his character development.

5. A mature Christian is generous. He is generous with his time and money because he is a steward and understands that he owns nothing but is responsible to

God for the possessions entrusted to him. Thus, he is free to share his resources, not anxious about personal provision because he knows God will provide.

6. *A mature Christian teaches others how to live a godly life.* This is not to say that he is a pastor or a Sunday school teacher, but that the way he lives and his familiarity with the truth of Scripture convinces others of the gospel. He is always prepared to talk about Jesus Christ with others, especially the lost.

7. *A mature Christian manages his areas of responsibility well.* If a father, he successfully cares for his family. On the job, he is dependable, honest, and hard-working. In the church, his word is rock-like, a word everyone has confidence in.

8. *A mature Christian knows how to obey.* This seems so simple, so obvious—but it is rarely seen among Christians today. Many

who want to obey God cannot take direction from brothers and sisters whom God has placed over them. The mature Christian is not threatened by godly authority, because he is submitted to Christ and secure under him.

9. A mature Christian knows how to relate well with brothers and sisters. He knows how to encourage and correct, how to repair wrongdoing, how to build relationships that last. He is marked by loyalty to brothers and sisters, always seeking their good. His tongue is under control; he is particularly careful to avoid slander and gossip. Maintaining the unity of the body of Christ is one of his highest priorities.

10. A mature Christian has personal spiritual disciplines in good order. He has a regular prayer life, knows Scripture, is free in his worship of God. In sum, he has an open, daily relationship with the

Father in which he submits every area of life to him.

One of the best-kept secrets of the Christian life is that it *is* possible, with God's help, to grow up before we grow old. Let's resolve to surrender our lives to the Great Discipler, and to cooperate fully with him in his work of molding us into the image and likeness of Jesus.